Football: Those Were The Days

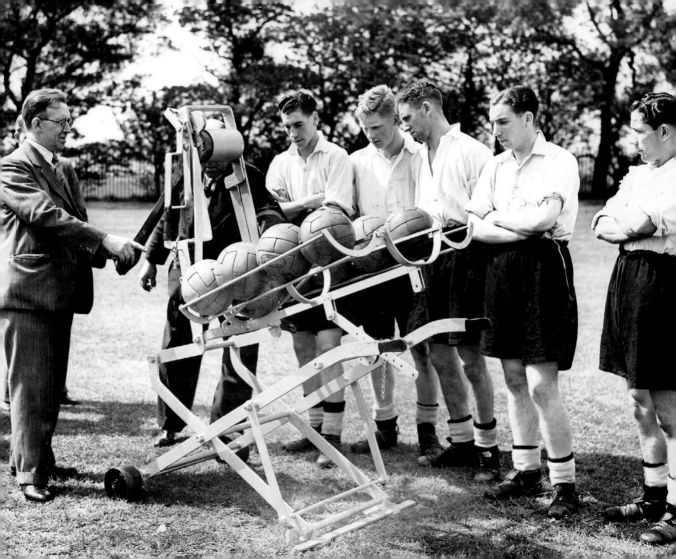

Football: Those Were The Days

Captain William Featherstone-Dawes

PORTICO

First published in the United Kingdom in 2011 by
Portico Books
10 Southcombe Street
London
W14 0RA

An imprint of Anova Books Company Ltd

ISBN 13: 978-1-907554-44-5

A CIP catalogue record for this book is available from
the British Library.

10 9 8 7 6 5 4 3 2 1

Reproduction by Rival Colour Ltd.
Printed and bound by 1010 Printing International Limited, China

This book can be ordered direct from the publisher.
Contact the marketing department, but try your bookshop first.

www.anovabooks.com

CONTENTS

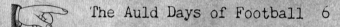

THE OLDE DAYS OF FOOTBALL

Football is the game of the people. We invented it. Nowhere is this more evident than in Lincolnshire where cheery labourers and local farmers take part in the annual "footballe matche".

Here they come across Old Muck Bridge, intent upon leathering the ball into the next field with a whoop and a hearty hobnailed wallop.

Opposed to them, and behind our camera, you can guarantee that there will be an equal number of ill-dressed labouring men attempting to do the same.

In the olde days it was village against village and at <u>Ashbourne</u> in Derbyshire the original game is played every Shrovetide. Those born north of the Henmore Brook are the Up'ards and those born south of it are the Down'ards.

The goalposts are three miles apart. One doesn't score a goal, one "goals a ball" by striking it against the mill stone three times. One is likely to hear many colloquial phrases uttered during the game including, "Down wi' it!" (play up Down'ards) and "'Ave ya seen ball, duck?" (where is the ball, friend?).

These regular mud larks from Leigh-on-Sea in Essex are playing the game at low tide at the start of the Leigh Regatta. Dressed in top hats and tails this is not a regular game of association football, though the playing surface looks very familiar.

A **celebratory drink** for the winners? No, this is merely the half-time bar. Mr. Goodwin, the Leigh skipper, pictured at right, is about to stir his team with a rousing half-time address. But first, here's mud in your eye!

OUR YOUNGSTERS LEARN THE GAME

Football captures the imagination of the young like nothing else. If they cannot be outside in the street playing it, why they'll be inside playing it. Here some youngsters are playing a terrific game of blow football. While some educationalists frown upon trivial diversions for the young, others point out that it is producing young fellows with prodigious lung capacity.

Let us hope someone cleans the table afterwards.

The love of football cuts across all **class** boundaries.
It's blazers-for-goalposts out on College Green for these
public school boys.

Strict **school rules** prevent them from removing
their caps, on punishment of a severe caning from their
housemaster. So, no **rip-roaring** celebrations, boys.
And Buttingford Minor, perhaps that wristwatch
should be given to **matron** for safekeeping.

These **working-class** lads are having a good old kickabout at the end of their street. The ball may have seen better days but the football-crazy lads couldn't care a jot.

They are too busy trying to emulate their heroes Stanley Matthews and Tommy Lawton with fantastic mazy dribbles. A **grazed knee** is a small price to pay for the honour of scoring the winning goal against Scragg Street.

Playing fields? Who needs playing fields when one can chalk out a goal on the wall at the end of one's two-up two-down terrace.

———⋙◦⋘———

The spirited young <u>East Ender</u> in the foreground is risking a fist in the old "boat race" with a brave header against a determined goalie.

———⋙◦⋘———

Both dream of playing for <u>Clapton Orient</u> one day. But if they smash a pane of glass instead, well they'll end up feeling a bit "tom and dick".

Not to be outdone, here's Bobby Charlton's mother, Cissie, getting stuck in during a friendly game with Bobby in the street.

───◄►○◄►───

Cissie is the cousin of the great Jackie Milburn as well as being the mother of rising Manchester United star Bobby. It looks like when it comes to a dangerous cross, mother knows best.

Play up Bobby!

This young lad is being taught one of the essential skills of the modern game, how to trap the ball with the boot, by Arthur Grimsdell of the Corinthians.

Trapping the ball with the boot affords players more control and is less exhausting than forever chasing after it. It is a difficult skill to achieve, but is much sought after by the progressive player.

Which aspiring forward would not want to exhibit
a mazy dribble to bamboozle the opposition's
wing halves? This skill requires intense
and unflinching concentration and a fine
coordination between eye and boot.

See how the younger players' gaze is fixed intently
upon the ball, fearful of missing the slightest
bobble. In time, the dribble will come naturally to
them, but many hours of practice are required before
they can exhibit an acceptable level of control
and maziness.

Boys of <u>Stepgate School</u>, Chertsey are all football enthusiasts and amongst their ranks may be the soccer stars of the future. Their sports master Eric Thomas considers the throw-in one of the most important aspects of the game.

This he teaches them by lining his class up, smallest in front and tallest at the back, and instructing them en masse. Stepgate may not have a junior league-winning side this season, but their throw-ins are the tops.

The old adage goes: If you can't beat 'em, join 'em.

Billy Pethers of Hammersmith must be London's luckiest schoolboy as he has been chosen as one of the six ball scouts for the cup final on Saturday.

Here his Latimer Road schoolmates give him a rousing send-off.

Billy is noted for his fine football skills and his small stature acts in his favour as he will not obstruct the spectators' view when running along the touchline.

RADIO SERVICE

TRAIN HARD, PLAY HARD

Is it a chorus line? No. The very best association football teams are employing some intense training methods to keep their players at their physical peak. An exponent of the new calisthenics is Mr. A. W. Douglas of Sheffield Wednesday. Under his stern tutelage the players are put through a rigorous workout before a ball is kicked. See how he reprimands the slacker who has his knee too low.

"Keep 'em up boys and we'll win that first division trophy!" he is saying.

Surely training shouldn't be this much fun? The Chelsea players are in very merry mood as they take part in exercises at Stamford Bridge. But these games have a secret purpose.

Not only do they provide energetic exercise, they build companionship and team spirit. Players learn to cope with unexpected happenings, like a stumble. Either that or we have stumbled upon plans to turn the Bridge into a holiday camp!

What a **circus** this football is! Many teams walk
a tightrope in their bid to avoid relegation, but at
Charlton Athletic it is the players who must keep their
nerve and their balance.

The players are encouraged to hone their **balancing**
skills by walking down a length of drainage pipe placed
between two crates. Some find it tricky, while others,
such as Watson in the **white knickers**, find it a
walk in the park. What's next for our top soccer teams -
a high-wire act at half-time?

And look, Mr. Douglas's training techniques have begun to be copied elsewhere, in this instance at Queen's Park Rangers.

While some take to the new exercise with vigour, others, such as wing half Bain, can hardly muster the enthusiasm.

 Two laps of the pitch for you, sir!

We know that **apprentices** are getting younger by the year, but that chap at the back seems particularly young!

The cheeky interloper at <u>Manchester United's</u> training ground is getting some of the best training hints and tips in the business as he **squats** down next to the likes of <u>Charlton</u> and <u>McGuinness</u>.

We've heard of the famous **Busby babes**, but this might be taking things a little too far...

Training is blooming marvellous at Crystal Palace
these days! We're glad to say that the Eagles'
supporters don't let the grass and the flowers
grow under their feet.

These chaps have resumed training ahead of the new
season and the groundsman must be off on a very
long holiday.

Or perhaps Palace want to emulate London rivals
Chelsea and have their own flower show.

Talking of the Blues, Weaver, Chelsea wing half, throws a ball further than anyone else in football.

———•○•———

He can place the ball on a 6d more than halfway across the field when standing on the touchline - a really polished footballer.

His team-mates can only stand back and watch in admiration as he focuses his full attention on the throw. 'How does he do it?' They all ask.

Deception is an important part of association football. There is the **wizardry** of the mazy dribble and there is also the cunning guile of the swerve.

No need to shoulder charge the full back when a crafty **swerve** will get you past a player. Here Mr. O'Neill the well-known North-East football personality is demonstrating the swerve to a group of players at West Ayton.

That **dropped shoulder** is the key move, get it right and you're half way there.

'Technology too plays its part in the modern game. The players of Wolverhampton are introduced to Robot Football Mate, a revolutionary new machine that will aid training.

Instead of good old Bill sending over a low cross, a high cross, a long cross and then a short cross, Robot Football Mate can send over the same cross four times in a row. Soon, every club will have one.

Training need never be muddy again. The gymno
frame is an all-British product made of tensile steel
tubes by which physique and balance can be maintained
and strengthened. Soon, every club will have one. Here
it is demonstrated to the Arsenal players in their
gymnasium at Highbury.

———◦◦◦———

The question is, are the players as
interested in the invention as much as
they are in the pretty young slip of
a demonstrator?

☞ Come, on you Gunners, "Atten-shun!"

AND SO TO THE GAME

A charming aspect of the modern game is the club mascot. As the Southampton team stride out onto the pitch at The Den, a young Southampton supporter dressed as a lucky black cat approaches the Southampton skipper, Keeping.

She hands him a lucky horse shoe. It is to wish the team luck in their cup tie against Millwall.

They are studiously ignored by Allen, the keeper.

Hoi, don't tug my tail! <u>Millwall</u> is
also the home of a larger member of the cat family
who prefers his tail not to be tugged. And what better
place to find a lion than in the <u>Den</u>.

The splendid and realistic costume of the Millwall
lion is a familiar sight on the terraces at home
games. The big cat does his best to rally cries of
"Play up Millwall". How he loves to hear the fans roar.

Mascots are a popular addition to the game. Down in the valleys, Swansea City's mascot turns out in traditional Welsh costume of hat, shawl and laverbread.

Cerys Jones, a pupil at Sketty Methodist Infant School, leads her beloved white Swans onto the pitch. Play up you Swans and let us see those feet a paddlin' up and down the pitch.

Come rain or shine the **professional** footballer will turn out every Saturday to entertain the fans. But it looks like the tide is in for this cup fixture at Rootshall between <u>Southend United</u> and <u>Manchester City</u>.

The Manchester players are certainly used to a bit of rain, but pity the poor fans with no stand above them. Ah well, even more excuse for a hot pie at half-time and a cheering ale. The fans might try that, also.

Ah, the hardy resilience of the British goalie. His job of work may be defending a **small puddle**, but what a magnificent job he does.

———⊷◈⊷———

The ability to adapt to changing conditions makes our goalies the best in the world. Does this chap look downcast at the prospect of spending 90 minutes having a bit of a **paddle**? No. It's dry up the other end...

The captains of Chelsea and Birmingham City meet in the centre circle to shake hands and exchange pennants.

———◆◦◆———

Now the referee presides over the coin toss. Wilson, the Birmingham City captain, is such an energetic tosser that the coin has disappeared out of the top frame of our photograph.

———◆◦◆———

But for the record he called heads correctly.

'This is the face of modern association football.

Grounds are beginning to resemble advertising hoardings with high-profile advertisers taking their pick of the best sites.

With players' demands to scrap the £17 per week maximum wage limit, the pressure is on for clubs to make money any way they can. What's next, you say, 'Smoke Capstan Cigarettes' printed on the back of the FA Cup...?

RADIO SERVICE

'That was a close one! Fairbrother, the experienced Newcastle goalie, leaps into the air to see the ball narrowly scrape the post and go dead.

'The modern keeper must be both agile and sturdy enough to withstand a centre forward's shoulder charge. Fairbrother is both.

Looking at that leap it's no surprise the Geordies have nicknamed him 'Jack the Cat'.

The keeper's not so lucky this time.

The defenders can only stand and stare as the ball hurtles into the back of the net.

—◆◆○◆◆—

Look as much as you like, chaps, your glances won't draw it back out.

That's a goal, that is.

"Mr. Linesman! Are you entirely certain I was in an offside position? Do you by any chance need spectacles?"

Sad to say this is another regrettable aspect of the modern game. The Corinthian spirit of "play up and play the game" is disappearing.

The **referees' association** must move swiftly to counter this slide into anarchy. "Any more of your cheek sonny and your name will be in the referee's notebook!"

Here's a fellow we like the look of. Mr. Nattras of Sealham will stand no nonsense from the crowd at St. Mary's.

"Any more of this foul language," he lectures them, "and I'll have the whole terrace cleared."

The message is plain. Cheer on your own team by all means, but do not denigrate the visiting side. Three cheers for Mr. Nattras for insisting on fair play.

After a tough game on the pitch what better way to
soothe the muscles than in a relaxing bath.

⟫⟩•⟨⟪

These Brentford players may be a little cramped sharing
four to a bath, but many managers believe it helps build
team spirit - you scrub my back, I'll scrub yours!

⟫⟩•⟨⟪

Let's hope no-one drops the soap.

Room for nine - that's luxury.

Ipswich Town players relax at Portman Road with a soak and a smoke.

These grand facilities may be reminiscent of a Turkish bath or a gentleman's club, but they are increasingly the norm at first- and second-division clubs.

Ooops!

This young lady's got more balls than she can handle.

Back to the locker room with them until the next game.

A word here about the footballer's haircut.

Many of our national newspapers exercise themselves greatly about the foppish nature of our leading players and what a poor example they give to the many schoolboys who follow the game.

Here we see the Southern Railway First XI. A finer body of well-groomed men you couldn't wish to set eyes upon. Apart from the fellow second left who has recently arrived from the moon.

A SUPPORTER'S LIFE FOR ME

Hats off to you fellows!

This good-natured crowd await a game between <u>Fulham</u> and <u>Everton</u> on the terraces of <u>Craven Cottage</u>.

Note how every single one of them is wearing a hat. Some wave their titfers while some have humorous and encouraging notes attached to the brims. Which we cannot read at this distance.

Boy coming down!

To the great amusement of all concerned, lads are
regularly passed over the heads of the crowd so
they can get a better view at the front.

Such is the terrific good nature of supporters
that they all willingly oblige.

Let's hope this young man remembered to keep his
thrupence ha'penny pocket money in a secure place!

At a <u>Wilmslow</u> factory, girls are engaged sewing numbers onto football jerseys - a terrific new scheme to make the game easier for spectators.

They will be able to identify their favourite players by way of number.

<u>Full backs</u> will have the numbers two and three; the wing halves, four and six, et cetera.

The coveted number will be the sharpshooting centre forward, number 11.

ENGLAND v SCOTLAND

1	3	5	7
2	4	6	8

RADIO SERVICE

The BBC is playing their part, too.
In future, radio commentary will announce
where the ball is to be found on the pitch,
using a scheme dividing the pitch into eight squares.

The chap with the alarming bandage is pointing at
Square One. This is where the ball is.

England will endeavour to move the ball up through
squares three, five, six, seven and eight to score a
goal. If the attack breaks down then England will be
forced to go back to Square Two.

Wot, no ticket? Then there's only one way to see the West Ham v Arsenal cup tie at Upton Park and that's to go over the fence.

West Ham's **security measures** are so lax that getting into their ground is as easy as **blowing bubbles**.

The Hammers' signature tune is "I'm forever blowing bubbles", a popular occupation for those in the East End.

The result of free admission, as well as turnstile men taking some extra cash, is that grounds are becoming dangerously crowded.

The crowd at this cup tie at Highbury between Arsenal and Aston Villa is spilling onto the pitch.

Police try their best to shepherd them off the pitch, but the club secretary, Mr. Routledge, fears they won't succeed.

 Maybe it's time to get some Gunners in, Mr. Routledge.

At Stamford Bridge things have got entirely out of hand
with over 100,000 supporters cramming into the ground.
The visiting side is Dynamo Moscow and spectators
are straying onto the pitch to catch a glimpse of the
much-vaunted Russians as they play a friendly match
against Chelsea.

It is one of the few occasions when it is good to see
the Russians attack on British soil. Given this sort
of welcome, we are sure the Russians will be invited
back soon.

Is nothing sacred? Bolton goalkeeper Pym punches clear in the <u>Cup Final</u> at the <u>Empire Stadium</u>, <u>Wembley</u>, as <u>West Ham</u> press.

An **immense crowd** watches the scene. Watching from above are supporters who have shinned up drainpipes to get a pigeon's-eye view from the stadium roof. That's what comes from having so many **scaffolders** support the game.

No pies for them at half-time, though.

 A crowd of **supporters** in merry mood.
These gooning <u>Gunners</u> fans are charging about
St. Pancras Station about to board the express
to Liverpool.

They delight in dressing in the most outlandish attire
and making a terrible racket wherever they go.

Although it might be **tiresome** to take a long journey
with them, their unflinching good humour often helps
save the day when fellow travellers tell them, "Hoi,
pipe down over there you rowdy lot!"

What the dickens are these chaps chanting? No more Latin prep? Hardly. These are football fans. They are more likely to be chanting "Veni Vidi Vici Oxford!"

For they are Oxford United's scholar fans about to board the train to London for an away match.

With their rough working men's garb, they are unlikely to be mistaken for Oxford dons, but who knows, their mortar boards might come in handy for laying some bricks along the way.

"All the nice girls love a sailor. All the nice girls love a tar." That's what they sing down Plymouth Argyle way. Like rivals Portsmouth, the Pilgrims have a big following in the navy and these two characters are doing their best to rally support.

And here's something you don't see every day. The local Chinese community wish luck upon the <u>Pilgrims</u> with a traditional <u>Chinese</u> flying lantern balloon released before the game. Nice idea Mr. Wu, but it'll never catch on, stick to window cleaning.

"Come on the Albion!"

This black country local isn't referring to Brighton and Hove when he yells "Come on the Albion" at the top of his lungs.

This is Mr. Atkinson the nationally-known supporter. So enthusiastic is Mr. Atkinson that he has hardly left his native West Bromwich for the Cup Final versus Sheffield Wednesday before he has started his rallying cry.

Fan or fanatic? You, the reader, decide.

'The rich harmonious tones of the **accordion** are a pleasure to the ear. These <u>Blackpool</u> fans are in exceptional good cheer as they congregate for a **sing-song** before their sixth round tie with <u>Fulham</u> at <u>Craven Cottage</u>.

And why shouldn't the Seasiders be in good spirit.

They have the **Wizard** of the **Dribble (Stanley Matthews)** in their side, their own home-made FA Cup and the easy ambience of a Parisian café.

No rattles, no scarves, but the vegetable gives these taffs away.

These three men, or 'boyos' as they prefer to be known, are up from the valleys to watch Wales play England in the Home Internationals.

If anybody needs a leek in a hurry, Dai, Huw and Roddery are happy to oblige.

There's lovely, isn't it.

Anybody guess where these chaps have come from? Here's a clue: some took the high road and some took the low road.

These are Scotch supporters wearing the traditional **three-haggis cap.** They have brought their own bagpipers to the match with <u>England</u> and an impressively large banner to stir the hearts of their players.

✦

You can bet the England crowd will be yelling good naturedly, **"Pipe down over there, Jock!"**

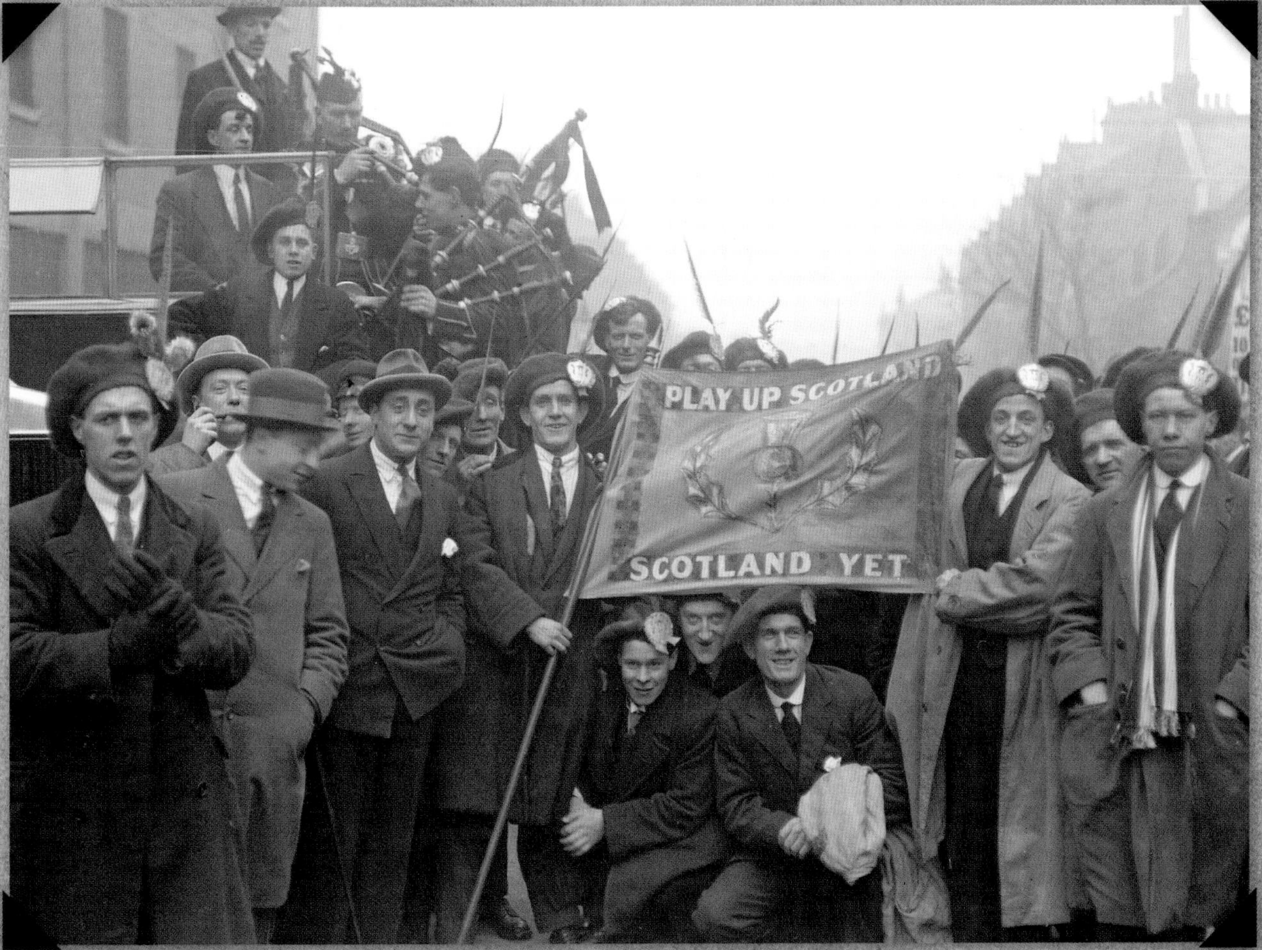
PLAY UP SCOTLAND
SCOTLAND YET

LADIES ATTEMPTING THE GAME

Two footballers **kissing**? Surely not. The trim ankles and marble-smooth porcelain thighs give them away, though. These are not <u>normal footballers</u>, but lady footballers exchanging pleasantries before a match.

Will you look at the priceless expression on the referee's face? He hasn't seen anything like it before either. He is doubtless thinking to himself, if this is before kick-off, what scene is going to unfold if they actually score a goal! That bucket of water on the touchline might come in handy!

Who says that golf gets all the stunners? These **adorable creatures** represent <u>Plymouth</u> in the newly formed Ladies' League <u>Division One</u>.

The Great War has knocked down barriers for **women and now shop assistants** and **dairy maids** can pitch up on a weekend and play the game that Britain gave the world.

They retain their femininity by the wearing of a comely bobble hat. Knitted themselves, of course.

These **Spanish senoritas** are used to playing their matches in a far warmer climate and are dressed for Madrid not Macclesfield.

Or should we say undressed. The rain in Spain may fall mainly on the plain, but they'll find that in England it rains every Saturday.

Those scraps of cloth covering their lower halves might survive a flamenco but not a muddy fracas in the six yard box.

They'll need stout boots, warm woolly socks and some long knickers wouldn't go amiss, miss.

They're a dab hand with the pots and pans
and a scrubbing brush, but can the feminine brain
understand the complexities of the offside rule?

Of course they can!

Here they listen to a detailed talk on the
offside trap while one lady points to a part
of the pitch that hasn't been ironed correctly.

Ladies can be some of the most ardent supporters of a team.

They show phenomenal loyalty.

This supporter of <u>Banstead Athletic</u> has sewn the famous 'Latics' XI onto her tight-fitting sweater in an attempt to ginger up the team.

The Banstead team have had the same starting line-up for three and a half years, a record only broken when wing half George Corbett was taken into hospital with typhus.

Fancy a pint and a pie at half-time?

Not this lot.

Adding a touch of glamour and sophistication to the supporters' ranks are the wives and girlfriends of the Norwich City first team. No dreary scarves or pinnies on display among this fashion-conscious group. With their head-turning model good looks they are the envy of every woman in the stadium. Eyes on the pitch, fellas!

Saints alive, June is busting out all over!

That's Connecticut-born June Neiffenecker, lead cheerleader of the True Blues, the new Birmingham City cheerleading team.

The football club are experimenting with Yankee-style cheerleaders to rally their supporters at St. Andrews. By the looks of it, June could use a little support herself.

YOU DON'T SEE THAT EVERY DAY

What kind of monkey business is this?

These squaddies from the army football team are getting a lesson in tactics from Jimmy the Chimp.

As long as they beat the navy, they couldn't "give a monkey's" who's in charge.

———◆◇◆———

At four-bananas-a-match he's a lot cheaper than most league managers and his post-match comments are always entertaining.

Meet Rex, the pools wonder dog.

Rex's uncanny knack of picking the right results has got the pools experts stumped and his owner, Mr. Billington, delighted.

For three successive Saturdays, Rex has scored six out of six correct outcomes in the football league.

With that kind of money, Mr. Billington, you can splash out on a carpet that reaches all the way to your skirting. And give old Rex a bone from us.

Is it a giant goalie? No.

These are comic circus midgets from the
Moscow State Circus.

They don't stand a chance heading the ball against
Barfield, Fulham's full-sized keeper, but what a laugh
they're all having. They are brought together by the
common language of football, a language that the British
gave the world.

White Hart Lane enjoys a prestigious visit from a German international XI. After an impromptu knockabout between the trenches during the Great War our two great nations always enjoy a friendly soccer match. How tall do you think your Führer is, chaps...?

And here's their **team coach** turned up early.
Plenty of space in the car park, Ferdinand.

From Germans who love football, to a footballer who
loves Germans, the sporting Prince of Wales is
in the thick of the action yet again as he kicks off
at a charity football match near Ascot.

———◦———

Not long until you put the No. 8 shirt on yourself,
your highness.

She may come all the way from China but when Chi-Chi the panda isn't chewing bamboo shoots, she likes nothing better than a kick-about with her keeper Mr. Pringle.

——◆◇◆——

As Mr. Pringle humorously puts it, she eats shoots and leaves and shoots.

"Have a lovely day at work, Daddy." That's <u>Chelsea</u> centre forward **Roy Bentley** waving goodbye to his lovely wife and daughter as he sets out from their charming suburban home.

But why hasn't Daddy gone to Stamford Bridge? With training only three days a week, Roy has time to pursue a career in stationery sales. He shows his latest range of cards and gift items to a West London tobacconist. There'll be no sale here. He's a Tottenham supporter.

"I say, that looks rather like the FA Cup on the front of that charabanc." That's because it is.

The Spurs decided to show off their newly won trophy on a triumphant return through the streets of Tottenham to White Hart Lane.

They received rapturous applause and many choruses of "for they are jolly good fellows". Luckily for them the famous lid stayed on when the driver hit an enormous pothole at Manor Lane.

My word, that's a **whopper**.

And a **tiddler**, too!

They are both produced by the Pukka sporting goods firm to demonstrate their expertise in leather craftsmanship.

They were due to display a similarly sized boot, but an old woman has taken up residence in it! What a hoot. At least referees won't need **spectacles** to see this **ball** go over the line!

There may be a net involved, but it is football girls, <u>not netball</u>. Shapely lingerie models don't make the best footballers but with a bit of training they can soon be licked into shape.

 Good show! A firm header will soon see the danger cleared. Best to leave the lesson about controlling it on the chest till next time.

PHOTOGRAPH ACCREDITATION

We are most obliged to the following photographic bureaus for their assistance in providing images of the highest quality for this work. In particular to Mr. Luigi Di Dio of the Getty Archives of Maida Vale, London, who furnished us with black and white photographs for the following pages: 8, 10, 11, 16, 19, 23, 24, 26, 29, 31, 33, 36, 40, 43, 45, 46, 49, 51, 52, 55, 61, 73, 75, 76, 79, 80, 83, 85, 86, 88, 91, 95, 96, 98, 100, 101, 103, 105, 106, 109, 111, 112, 115, 116, 119, 122, 136, 137 and 139.

Thanks also to Mr. John Moelwyn-Hughes of Corbis Images, who furnished plates for the following pages: 7, 15, 58, 128, 133, 134 and 140.

We are also most grateful to Mr. David Scripps of Mirrorpix who supplied pictures for pages 12, 20, 34, 39, 62, 64, 120, 125, 126, 131, 142 and 143.

And finally to Mr Atkinson of Rex Features who facilitated plates for pages 56, 66, 68, 92 and 130.

Photographic research: Frank Hopkinson

Design: Claire Marshall

Layout: Sarah Rock